HAFIZ OF SHIRAZ

HAFIZ OF SHIRAZ

Thirty Poems

An Introduction to the Sufi Master

Translated by

Peter Avery
and
John Heath-Stubbs

HANDSEL BOOKS
an imprint of
Other Press • New York

Copyright © 2003 Peter Avery and John Heath-Stubbs

Book design: Kaoru Tamura

Production Editor: Robert D. Hack

This book was set in Sabon by Alpha Graphics of Pittsfield, NH.

10 9 8 7 6 5 4 3 2 1

All rights reserved. No part of this publication may be reproduced or transmitted in any form or by any means, electronic or mechanical, including photocopying, recording, or by any information storage and retrieval system without written permission from Other Press LLC, except in the case of brief quotations in reviews for inclusion in a magazine, newspaper, or broadcast. Printed in the United States of America on acid-free paper. For information write to Other Press LLC, 307 Seventh Avenue, Suite 1807, New York, NY 10001. Or visit our website: www.otherpress.com.

Library of Congress Cataloging-in-Publication Data

Ḥāfiẓ, 14th cent.
[Dīvān. English. Selections]
Hafiz of Shiraz : thirty poems : an introduction to the Sufi master / translated by Peter Avery and John Heath-Stubbs.–2nd ed.
p. cm.
Originally published: Thirty poems. 1st ed. London : J. Murray, 1952, in series: Wisdom of the East series.
ISBN 1-59051-070-4
I. Avery, Peter, 1923-   II. Heath-Stubbs, John Francis Alexander, 1918-
III. Ḥāfiẓ, 14th cent. Thirty poems. IV. Title.
PK6465.Z31A9 2003
891'.5511–dc21   2003003796

CONTENTS

Foreword	vii
Acknowledgments	xiii
Introduction	1
Translations	23
Glossary of Names	75
Notes	79

FOREWORD

In 1947–1948, when I was studying Persian and beginning to read Hafiz at the University of London School of Oriental and African Studies, I was approached by an already established British poet, John Heath-Stubbs, who wanted to know what the famous Persian poet said. I began a series of translations of Hafiz's lyrics, rendered as literally from the Persian as the English idiom could bear. The aim was to reflect as precisely as possible the sense of the originals. All English "poetical" embellishments were to be avoided, so that the enamel-like hardness of the Persian poems could be displayed.

From the eighteenth century onward, with Sir William Jones's inclusion in his *Persian Grammar* of a Hafiz translation, "The Fair Maid of Shiraz" (our Number VII), Hafiz had been a subject of interest to British men of letters. Beckford, for example, reports that in Madrid in 1798 he had two conversations with the Turkish Ambassador to the Spanish court about Hafiz. Officers of the East India Company during the same period are described as comparing Horace with Hafiz over breakfast. Consequently, in the nineteenth century numerous translations of Hafiz's poems were published.[1] In 1901 John Payne published three volumes of the poems of Hafiz. As Arberry says, "His picture of Hafiz was certainly not lacking in sentimentality." Less twee were the attractive translations of Gertrude Bell (London 1897). From 1845 E. B. Cowell, who began to teach Edward FitzGerald Persian in 1852, started publishing Hafiz's lyrics in English in literary magazines, generally in prose versions. FitzGerald responded by saying, "Your Hafiz is fine; and his tavern world is a sad and just idea!" FitzGerald, famous for his version of the *Ruba'iyat of Omar Khayyam*, later commented that Hafiz was of "true metal," but too difficult to translate. Interesting is the fact that FitzGerald showed Hafiz's poems in translations to Tennyson, who, according to FitzGerald, took "some interest." But for neither Tennyson nor Carlyle, to whom FitzGerald also showed English versions of Hafiz, did

---

1. For an account of these translators, see A. J. Arberry, *Classical Persian Literature*, London, 1958, Chapter 13.

the great and varied Persian lyricist become the obsession of a lifetime that he became for Goethe, as part of Goethe's far-reaching interest in Persian literature in general, an interest that began in 1814 after Joseph von Hammer-Purgstall published his German prose version of Hafiz's collected poems. Goethe was inspired by Hammer-Purgstall's translation to imitate Hafiz's Ghazals, publishing his *Westöstlicher Divan* in 1819.

It will be clear that in Europe and not least Great Britain, Hafiz was considered a highly attractive proposition by literary people up to the 1920s. Alas, in respect of this great poet, times have changed. But in 1952 when John Heath-Stubbs and I published our version of the Ghazals, which are now being reissued, we were aware of Emerson's dictum that Hafiz was "a quarry of imagery in which poets of all ages might mine," and we were motivated by the desire to issue a sort of manifesto on the subject of translation from the Persian. Paramount in our plan was the rejection of the translator's "improvements," of the translator's assumption that he might know better than the poet what the poet intended to say, and of the type of ornament, applied at the expense of accuracy, characteristic of Payne's work. As alluded to above, our purpose was to convey that hardness of the Persian lyric, which is totally devoid of the misty whimsicality with which English translations have tended to endow it. As for rhyme and metrical devices, while a certain rhythm in the lines was sought, an arrangement that would result in a jingle was rigorously excluded. After all, great and strong poetry can come through a prosaic rendering, as the Hebrew Psalms in the Authorized Version of the Bible prove.

It is not intended here to rewrite the original Introduction, but it might be said that the statement about Hafiz's religion, that he was a Shi'ite, now fifty years later might seem—though it has been attested by at least one eminent Iranian scholar—too dogmatic. Nobody really knows for sure what Hafiz's "religion" was, but he was, above all, a Sufi, and to be a Sufi is to be above the differences and squabbles of religious divisions. It is also clear that he was far from being orthodox: near-contemporary historians record at least one incident in which he was chastised by his sovereign prince for a seemingly heterodox statement in a verse that he cleverly contrived to alter, and so make less offensive to more fanatical Muslims. His resentment at the severe application of Islamic prohibition of the use of wine is apparent in practically every poem he uttered.

It is important that a poet who has remained immensely popular and most frequently quoted in his own land should, for the universality and grace of his wisdom and wit, be known outside the land of his birth as he used to be, the subject of veneration among literati in both Europe and the United States. The time for revival of interest in a poet of such cosmopolitan appeal is overdue.

Peter Avery
August 2002

ACKNOWLEDGMENTS

Acknowledgments are due to Professor A. J. Arberry's *Fifty Poems of Hafiz* (Cambridge University Press, 1947). We have extensively used the Persian text there given, and the editor's valuable introduction and notes. Other editions of Hafiz's poems consulted include the *Diwan-i-Hafiz* of Major W. S. Jarrett (Calcutta, 1881), which follows the order given in the Brockhaus edition (Leipzig, 1854); the Divan edited by Rosenzweig-Schwannau (Vienna, 1858–1864), with his German translation; and the Tehran edition (1941) of Mirza Muhammad Qazvini and Dr. Qassim Ghani. The order of the poems, and the numbering printed in roman figures at the head of each of the present translations, is that of the Brockhaus edition.

Extensive use has been made of John Payne's industrious *Poems of Shamseddin Mohammed Hafiz of Shiraz, Done into English* (Villon Society, 1901), and reference has also been made to the translation of Justin MacCarthy (1893), while an eye has always been kept on the *Poems from the Divan of Hafiz* (1897) of Gertrude Bell, whose excellent notes and introduction have been a fruitful source of information.

We wish especially to thank G. M. Wickens, M.A., formerly Lecturer in Persian and Arabic at the School of Oriental and African Studies (University of London) and now University Lecturer in Arabic at Cambridge, for his constant help and encouragement. Many of the arguments advanced in our Introduction owe their inception to Mr. Wickens and have been put forward by him in his lectures. This is particularly the case in regard to the theory of the colloquial nature of much of Hafiz's style, and to the historical and social causes suggested for this; and also as concerns our whole approach to the formal analysis and image-structure of the poems.

Mention should be made of Harold Nicolson, for his interest in our efforts, and of G. H. Darab, of the London School of Oriental Studies, for his great encouragement of the English student of his own language. Thanks are also due to many friends, especially Hugh Gordon Porteous, George Barker, and David Wright, who have given encouragement and criticism to these translations, considered as English poems.

J. H.-S.
P. W. A.

INTRODUCTION

Shams ud-Din Muhammad, known as Hafiz, was born at Shiraz, the capital of the province of Fars, in Persia, some time after A.D. 1320, and died there in 1389. He is thus an almost exact contemporary of our Chaucer. Very little is really known about his life. For the various picturesque legends that formed about his name in later times, the reader is referred to Gertrude Bell's *Poems from the Divan of Hafiz* (1897). He will there learn how Hafiz was said miraculously to have received the gift of poetry from Khizr, a mysterious personage of Near Eastern folklore—a sort of scholar-gypsy, who had discovered the Elixir of Life, and who appeared from time to time to ordinary mortals; and of the interview Hafiz is related to have had with the conqueror Timur, who certainly entered Shiraz during the poet's lifetime. The *takhallus*, or pen name,

Hafiz means "one who can recite the Koran by heart." Hafiz makes more than one reference to the duties that this, his profession, entailed. We also know that he lectured, in Koranic exegesis, in a *madrassa*, or mosque school, in his native city.

Hafiz lived in the "time of troubles" of the Iranian civilization. After the collapse of the Il-Khans, cities like Shiraz, falling prey to the ambitions of one marauding prince after another, knew little peace. Further, the nomads of Central Asia represented a continual threat. Their power, organized by Timur, whose invasions were carried out with great ruthlessness and cruelty, was finally to overthrow entirely the rule of these princes, and to lead to the establishment of the succeeding Timurid dynasty.

Like all the Persian poets of the Middle Ages, Hafiz was a court poet and a panegyrist, dependent on the good will of his patron. In 1353 Abu Ishaq Inju, at that time ruler of Shiraz, was overthrown by Mubariz ud-Din Muhammad, the Muzaffarid. The latter took Shiraz in November of that year and a hard time for this sophisticated city ensued, for Mubariz was a stern fanatic and, among other things, forbade the sale of wine. In 1358, however, he was deposed by his more amiable son, Jalal ud-Din Shah Shuja', under whose patronage, with the help of his minister Hajii Qavam ud-Din, Hafiz obtained the professorship in Koranic exegesis in a madrassa. It is impossible to say how much these dynastic revolutions affected Hafiz personally. We can detect in his poetry, however, many references to the world's ingratitude, as well as to the intrigues and slanders of his rival poets, and more or less pointed appeals to the generosity of patrons.

The work of Hafiz is remarkably colloquial in its tone. During his lifetime it circulated widely—and still retains an extensive popular currency—in all those countries where Persian was employed as a literary language. He received invitations to visit the courts of rulers as far removed as Baghdad and the Deccan, but declined to leave his native city. This currency of his poetry was mainly oral, though it is said that he compiled a Divan, or Collected Works, during his own lifetime. This collection, however, if the tradition is true, had been lost by the time of his death, and his poems were collected by his friend Muhammad Gulandam.

Hafiz was by religion a Muslim of the Shi'a. Shi'ism, which in later times, in its less extreme form, was to become the state religion of Persia, was then still the doctrine of a minority—though an important and widely dispersed one—in the Muslim world. In contradistinction to the orthodox or Sunni party, the Shi'a based its position on the claim that 'Ali, Muhammad's son-in-law and cousin, and his descendants, had possessed an inalienable divine right of succession to the Caliphate.

Fundamentally, however, the significance of Shi'ism is more far-reaching than that of a quarrel as to legitimacy, and proximity to the Person of the Prophet, among his successors. On the one hand, Shi'ism represented the reaction of the non-Arab peoples of the lands subdued by the early Islamic conquests against their Arab overlords, while, on the other, as in the course of time the Abbasid Empire developed, it became a rallying point for all those with social grievances. Their hopes were projected upon the figure of the unjustly dispossessed 'Ali, his martyred sons Hasan and Husain, and their successors, designated Imams, who could likewise be represented as martyred and passively suffering figures. Doubtless these Shi'a saints attracted to themselves many of the attributes of the older suffering and dying divine figures of the Near East. In Shi'a theology there appears to be a considerable undercurrent of pre-Islamic ideas. Muhammad and 'Ali are conceived of as more than merely human figures; they are overshadowed by the divine radiance of Ahura Mazda. The number of the legitimate Imams, estimated by the schools having the more extreme tendencies as seven, and by milder adherents of the Shi'a as twelve, has also its significance in relation to the ancient astrological religion of Babylon—which survived at Harran (on the border between Persia and Iraq) until well into the Middle Ages.

Shi'ism, attracting as it did Arabophobes and the socially discontented, frequently assumed a politically activist form—the movement of the Assassins is a notable example of this. Its tenets, particularly those of "the Seveners," combined with what had come down from earlier Near Eastern doctrines (such as, for instance, the sanctity of the number seven), the ancient Iranian idea of divine light, already referred to, Gnostic speculations and Greek and Manichaean elements. Thus it formed an esoteric doctrine, which fell on ground fertile for the formation of secret societies, toward which a strong inclination may be presumed to have long existed in the East from ancient times. One of the earliest literary expressions of these extreme elements in Shi'ism were the writings of "The Brethren of Purity," compiled in Iraq in A.D. 763. By 890 it definitely emerged as a serious politically subversive movement under a leader called Hamdan Qarmat. In view of its persistence, under different guises, the possibility that Hafiz (who lived in a disrupted age, but who was himself of the more moderate "Twelver" sect) might sometimes have used his poetry, with its studied obliquities and ambiguities of phrase, to address a secret sect of initiates should perhaps be taken into account. It is nevertheless a fact that any poet always, in a sense, does address a "set of initiates," and, in this connection, one is reminded of a beautiful story, the tenth in the

Second Book of the *Gulistan* of Hafiz's famous fellow citizen, Sa'adi. In this story the poet describes how he was addressing an unappreciative audience, upon which his words had no effect. He was, moreover, speaking on a text in the Koran of considerable import to the Sufis (Surah L, verse 15): "We created man, and we know what his soul whispereth within him; and we are nearer unto him than his jugular vein," from the words of which he had made a couplet (extremely beautiful in the Persian) that may be literally translated as follows:

> The Friend is nearer to me than I am myself: this is puzzling—
> I am far from Him.
> What can I do? To whom can I tell that He is in my breast and
> I am cut off from Him?

He was, he continues, "drunk with the wine of these words," when suddenly a shout arose from someone passing by on the fringe of that apathetic audience, and the poet was moved to say: "Praise be to God! Those afar who know are near; and those near but without discernment, are afar." Further, the type of study to which the Shi'is subjected the Koran, in order to discover internal meanings within its every utterance, from which to justify their doctrines, must also be kept in mind when we consider the possible ingenuities of meaning in the work of a poet who surely inherited much from previous centuries of a surpassingly subtle intellectual activity.

There is, however, another religious force that underlies not only the poetry of Hafiz but practically all the lyrical poetry of Persia in the Middle Ages. This force is Sufism. Sufism was a mystical movement, which had emerged in Islam as early as the time of Hasan al-Basri, one of its first outstanding figures, who died in A.D. 728. It developed, significantly, as the times grew increasingly hard on the large mass of the people, and tensions of every sort came into being, during the dissolution of Abbasid power in the ninth and tenth centuries A.D. By the fourteenth century it had acquired an elaborate and conventional system of symbolism, which forms the stock-in-trade of poetic imagery. The tendency of Sufism is pantheistic. Each human soul is a particle of the divine Absolute, and the mystic aims at a complete union with the Divine. This union is attained in the knowledge that he is himself that ultimate Reality that he seeks. But the individual self is completely annihilated in this higher Self, like the moth drawn to the candle flame. For the sake of this esoteric knowledge, the Sufi must abandon all, in particular the legalistic restraints of conventional religion. In the eyes of the world he will appear a reprobate (there was a sect of extremists call the *Malamatiya*, the Reproached or Reprehensible), for his life is hidden with God.

The sources of Sufism, outside the Islamic tradition itself, are debatable. As far as Persia was concerned, however, it must be remembered that in the period immediately preceding the Muslim conquest, this country was open to the influence of various types of religious thought. These included the state Zoroastrian or Magian worship, Nestorian Christianity, Greek Neo-Platonism, and Indian Buddhism. When the Arabs conquered Persia in the seventh century, they took over a civilization much older and more complex than their own. Many of its elements undoubtedly persisted and found, as already suggested in connection with Shi'ism, an outlet in such mystical and esoteric religious movements as later appeared.

It is well known that orthodox Islam forbids the use of wine or any other intoxicants. Wine has the property of loosening the unconscious forces within ourselves, and in certain states of drunkenness it is possible to experience something bordering on ecstasy, in which we appear to have knowledge of a reality beyond the personal. From early times intoxicants have been used (as in the Greek Dionysiac cult) to produce artificially a state of religious ecstasy—as have other narcotics, notably, in the Near East, hashish. The use of wine, furthermore, has religious associations of another kind. The ancient Zoroastrian religion made use of an intoxicating liquor, *Hayyuma*, in its sacrificial rites, and wine is also used sacramentally by Christians.

It was natural, therefore, that for the Sufi poets wine should stand as the symbol of esoteric knowledge. As it was forbidden to orthodox Muslims, its sale passed largely into the hands of representatives of the older religions. The term *Magian*, therefore, became synonymous with wine-seller—though in practice these were often Christians or Jews, as well as Zoroastrians. The wine-shop becomes a "Magian temple"—and indeed such a place might well be the rendezvous of an esoteric circle or of a proscribed religion, in which intellectual intercourse between Muslims and non-Muslims would be possible. The Tavern keeper is the "Magian Elder," the archetypal Ancient Sage, dispenser of secrets, and the Sufi poet represents himself as his initiate and pupil. The cup that he holds in his hand is the magic cup of Jamshid, the mythical king and culture hero of the Golden Age of Iranic legend, to whom the invention of wine was ascribed. His cup reflects in its depths the whole world, and confers all knowledge on those who drink of it.

Although, as has been said, Sufi sources outside Islam are extremely debatable, it is not improbable that it was from the Neo-Platonist tradition that the Sufis adopted the conception of the Divine as Absolute Beauty, of which all images of beauty to be discerned in the natural world are partial and fleeting representations. This led to the formulation of a conception of romantic love, the germ of which is to be found in Diotima's speech to Socrates in Plato's *Symposium*. It is highly probable that Arabic love poetry, which belongs to the same tradition as the Persian, strongly influenced the romantic love poetry of the Provencal and early Italian poets. At any rate, there are many parallels, both in form and imagery, between Medieval European and Islamic (including Persian) lyrical poetry. For the Persians, however, as for the Greeks, the earthly expression of that Divine Beauty which the lover contemplates is embodied primarily in the form of a beautiful youth. The Beloved celebrated by Hafiz and the other Sufi poets is a conventionalized and not an individual figure. His beauty is described in terms of a number of stock images: thus the rose always represents his face, the moon his cheeks or brow, the cypress his graceful form, and so on. A similar conventional symbolism marks all the use of natural imagery, as employed by the later Persian poets. The nightingale, hopelessly enamored of the rose, represents the lover, as does the violet, with its humble growth and mournful hue. The morning breeze is the messenger of

Love, bearing the scent of musk out of the beloved's tresses. The beloved is sometimes the seller of sweetmeats, and the poet an eloquent, sugar-loving parrot. However stylized this imagery may seem, it belongs to the universal symbolic language of poetry. We find a similar symbolism in Chinese poetry, and there are many parallels in European Medieval lyrics and in later folk song, in which the old tradition survives. Much of the poet's art consists in the ingenious recombinations and reapplication of these traditional symbols. The degree to which they become, in the hands of Hafiz, vivid, natural, and personal, is no small token of his genius.

Hafiz depended on an audience that took this traditional symbolism for granted, yet that was sufficiently sophisticated to appreciate subtleties and ingenuities of all kinds—irony, plays upon words, oblique references to the Koran and Muslim theology (and whatever esoteric elements there may be in his poetry, it is against this Koranic background that it must primarily be read), and similar references to the ancient Persian heroic legends recorded by Firdousi in his *Shah Nama*. Such an audience would, quite naturally and unselfconsciously, be capable of understanding a poem on several simultaneous levels of significance. This implies a habit of mind that is only to be found in a culture more intellectually unified than our own. But here again, the

European Middle Ages, with their theory of the four-fold allegorical interpretation of Scripture (a theory that Dante, for instance, quite naturally applied to the interpretation of his own poetry), provide a fruitful analogy. But we must understand by "allegory" something much more complex and psychologically subtle than what that word came to signify for the Renaissance and after—the merely intellectual and sometimes arbitrary substitution of one image for another for the sake of rhetorical effect.

Almost any poem of Hafiz can, in fact, be read on at least three levels of significance—though we may suppose that sometimes one, sometimes another, is uppermost in the poet's mind. In the first place, the poems may be taken at their face value as songs in celebration of love and wine. They express the happy and graceful sensuality of a civilization that had achieved a great degree of refinement and sophistication, and which, in spite of the sternness of the Muslim theology that was its background, allowed of a considerable freedom of manners. In addition to the eroticism of its themes, this poetry is pervaded by a sexual symbolism, which is the more apparent to those familiar with the overtones which the images and words carry in the Persian language. But at a further remove is the interpretation in terms of Sufi mystical theology. The images of

Hafiz's poetry are to be taken as applicable to the universal experiences of the mystic. The beloved becomes the Divine Lover; separation from Him, in its various degrees, is the Dark Night of the Soul, union with Him the mystic's ecstatic absorption in the Absolute. Oriental commentators, indeed, give a precise allegorical significance to every point that the poet enumerates in describing the beauty of his beloved. Thus the mole of the cheek signifies the point of Divine Unity, the beloved's curling locks are the glory which at once veils and reveals the splendor of God, and so on. Mysticism that employs an erotic imagery is, of course, not unknown to the West. We find it preeminently in the poetry of St. John of the Cross and the Spanish mystics, who, at least by way of Ramon Lull if not through other channels, owed much to the traditions of Arabic Sufism. But in Persian, such mysticism had become a recognized part of the entire tradition of lyrical poetry, so that a poet like Hafiz, who is primarily an artist and not a mystic, can sing of sacred and profane love simultaneously and unselfconsciously.

Third, we must consider Hafiz as a court poet and panegyrist. The enumeration of the beloved's charms and the complaints of his cruelty, which also described the Divine Beauty, and the soul's grief at separation from it, are further to be read as compliments to a princely patron's magnificence, or respectful reproaches to him for his tardiness in rewarding his poet's services. This is a level of interpretation even more difficult for the modern reader to appreciate, though the conditions of Renaissance despotism, with its patronage of the arts, produced something like it in our own poetry. The aging and domineering Queen Elizabeth was addressed by her poet-courtiers in terms in which the subject's loyalty, the lover's gallantry, and the religious exaltations of virginity are inextricably mingled. And who can disentangle the strands of personal passion and gratitude to a patron that go to make up Shakespeare's sonnets? It must be remembered that the princes who, together with their ministers, were the subjects of Hafiz's laudatory verse, were absolute rulers. They could claim, in some sort, to be God's vice-regents on earth, and the splendor of their own courts was an image of the glory that is on high.

Upward of six hundred poems are attributed to Hafiz. Of these the majority are classifiable as ghazals. The ghazal is a type of short lyrical poem, consisting of six to fifteen *baits*, or couplets. Each bait consists of two hemistichs. The hemistichs of the first bait rhyme, and the same rhyme is repeated throughout the poem in the second hemistich of each bait. The concluding couplet nearly always incorporates the name of the poet, who is referred to in the third person, as if by the singer who is reciting the poem. Each couplet embodies a single statement or idea, while the poem as a whole often appears to have little formal unity, except that provided by the meter and the monorhyme. This, however, is not really the case. It is a mistake to regard the poems of Hafiz as consisting of "orient pearls at random strung," to which critics have often likened them. But we have to do with a conception of form that knows nothing of the logical principle that a poem shall consist of beginning, middle, and end. This principle, which has been tacitly accepted by post-Renaissance European criticism until our own day, owes its primary inception to Aristotle, whose formulation of it was based on an analysis of the works of the Attic dramatists. But a different formal principle is to be found in the pre-Attic lyrical poetry of Greece, notably in the Odes of Pindar. Professor Gilbert Norwood demonstrated (in his *Pindar*, California University Press, 1945) that the poems of Pindar, long supposed to be lacking in any clear thematic unity, are really bound together by the symbolic unity of their leading images. A very similar principle is discernible in the poems of Hafiz. Each couplet is linked to others in the same poem by a leading image or idea, or by the repetition of a single word, though often in a varying sense. But the links are not necessarily explicit: they are often suppressed and dependent upon subconscious association. Sometimes a couplet is thus linked to the one that immediately succeeds it. More often, perhaps, it has a closer connection with the next couplet but one, so that the several couplets of the poem may be said to be linked alternatively. This latter characteristic produces something analogous to the "arabesque" principle in design, which is so eminently typical of Islamic art in general. Finally, the composition of the poem as a whole is circular rather than linear: a leading image or word in the first couplet is repeated or paralleled in the concluding one. This circular principle of composition finds an analogy in contemporary Persian miniature-painting. And indeed the whole nature of Hafiz's imagery, in its vivid sense of detail and of bright color alike, and in its subject matter (e.g., the fondness for the formal garden setting), offers many parallels to the art of the Persian miniaturists.

The principles on which the thematic material and the imagery of Hafiz's poetry are unified, may, perhaps, best be illustrated by giving a prose translation of the following representative poem, with an analysis which, though only superficial, will show how closely related each couplet is to what precedes and follows it:

1. I saw the green meadow of the firmament and the sickle of the new moon—
   I remembered my own tillage and the time of the harvest.

2. I said, "Of Fate, you were asleep and the sun has come up"—
   He replied, "In spite of all that has gone before, don't give up hope."

3. If you go pure and naked like the Messiah to heaven—
   From your lamp a hundred rays will reach the sun.

4. Don't rely on your star, that night-robber, because this impostor
   bore off the crown of Kaus and the belt of Kaikhosrou!

5. Though the earring of gold and ruby weighs down the ear,
   the term of beauty is transient: listen to good advice!

6. The evil eye be far from your mole because, on the chessboard of beauty,
   it moved a pawn that beats the moon and sun.

7. Say to the sky, "Don't put this tawdry grandeur up for sale because in love the harvest
   of the moon goes for a barley-grain and the vine of the Pleiades for two grains!"

8. The fire of religious zeal and hypocritical zeal will burn up the harvest of religion—

   Oh Hafiz, throw away this woolen habit and go!

Verse 1. The *mise en scène*—a field (the sky) and the sickle (the new moon). Reaping is immediately suggested; therefore, in the following hemistich, the poet naturally comes to thoughts of his own harvest (in imagery very familiar to the Christian). There is an atmosphere of quiet and contemplation, evoked by gazing on the vastness of the sky and conducive to meditation on a high spiritual theme; a note of elevation has at once been struck.

Verse 2. Exercised, as Hafiz apparently was, over the matter of predestination (thereby, perhaps, evincing the influence of old doctrines of the Elect), thoughts of his own harvest must be followed by an address to Fate, pointing to the sun (in contrast to the moon) that ripens the corn for reaping—this being a suppressed association, of a kind this poetry is full of. The sun reference incidentally serves to bring us back to the sky—.

Verse 3. And the sky, with its glory, the sun, comes to the fore in this stanza, as a splendid image of Heaven and its crowning glory, God, with whom the "reaped" soul is garnered. The Messiah, Jesus, regarded by Muslims as a saint, is the example of such a soul.

Verse 4. This takes us back to the theme of Fate again, in the reference, still quite in keeping with the astronomical imagery of the poem, to "your star." This "thief of the night" is not the sickle of the new moon, yet it too reaps: not souls, but the vainglorious things of this world; but the harvest theme is thus, on a sublunary plane as it were, kept up, serving the development of another subsidiary theme in the poem.

Verse 5. The harvest theme, this time not imagining the reaping of souls, but of the transient objects of this life, bursts out in splendor with the gold and ruby that weighs down the ear (as the ripe grains weigh down the cornstalk) and which must pass: while this passing, this ripening and falling, serves also the purpose of allegory for the major theme of the poem, the harvest of souls.

Verse 6. This prepares the way in taking our thoughts off earthly adornments to the small point, the mole on the countenance of True Beauty (whence Fortune's machinations be far), which in one move can transcend all the powers of the cosmos—influencing the rulers of fate (which provides an interesting sidelight on Hafiz's attitude toward predestination).

Verse 7. This brings out overtly again the harvest-imagery and puts the play of Fate in its place in a reference to the harvest that is the poem's main concern, the harvest of the spirit by the Supreme Spirit. We are back to verse 1 again.

Verse 8. The spiritual harvest will, however, be burned up by false suns, the false suns of the hypocrisy that holds sway in conventional religion: so the poet must throw off the cloak (i.e., the woolen habit adopted by Sufi devotees) of hypocritical zeal and go—along the hidden path that is the way to the granary of the truly seeking spirit. Thus we are back to the main subject of this contemplative poem, the poet's own salvation, in brooding over which, as he gazed at the sky, he began the poem. It is as if the necklace of images has at last been clasped, and the end gathered into the beginning, in a statement of definite clarity.

In this connection textual difficulties must be considered. There is always a measure of uncertainty as to whether the text which has come down to us is as Hafiz himself actually composed it. So far, however, from this invalidating such attempts at analysis as the above, an overall approach on these lines might, after the necessary research, be of value (as Professor Arberry has pointed out) in establishing which of the various versions of any given poem is the better text. For by such a method we gain a fresh insight into Hafiz's technique with imagery, as well as in other matters.

It must not be forgotten that these poems were intended not primarily to be read, but to be sung or recited to a musical accompaniment. Their art, however elaborate, is based upon improvisation. The Persian court poet was expected to produce impromptu verses at the orders of his patron. Those who know something of Spanish flamenco singing will be acquainted with a form of art in some respect analogous and that derives, ultimately, from the same Islamic tradition. The reader must suppose the pause between each couplet on the part of the instrumentalist. This pause would give the accomplished singer time to improvise his next couplet, or at least the appearance of improvisation would be retained.

In making an English translation much of the subtlety and the formal characteristics of the original, of necessity, have to be sacrificed. It is impossible to reproduce with effect either the monorhyme or the elaborate quantitative meters of the Persian. But the employment of the rhymed stanza-forms of traditional English verse inevitably leads to the imposition of formal conceptions that are, as shown above, alien to Oriental poetry. In the translations here offered to the reader, the couplet has been preserved as the essential unit of the poem's structure. Unrhymed verse, however, has been employed, based on a loose line of, generally, six stresses, which can be expanded and contracted as its content demands. It is hoped that the effect thus produced will be found not unmusical by the reader accustomed to the cadences of modern verse. Where it seemed helpful, individual poems have been prefaced by a short prose abstract of their leading themes. The comparative freedom afforded by the form here employed as a medium of translation makes possible the preservation of a greater degree of accuracy than could be attained were we forced to conform the sense of the originals to a superimposed metrical pattern. But we have above all striven to preserve the essential intimacy, and the colloquial turn of phrase, that are characteristic of Hafiz's poetry. If some, at least, of the following renderings can be read as poetry in their own right, and give pleasure as such, our labor will not have been wholly in vain.

John Heath-Stubbs
Peter Avery

TRANSLATIONS

I

(He tells of the difficulties of love's way. The experienced guide knows that we must abandon reason to traverse its stages. Love begins with desire for self-gratification, and leads to ignominy. But by continual perseverance, that may be attained for which the world is well lost.)

Boy, bring the cup, and circulate the wine:
How easy at first love seemed, but now the snags begin.

How many hearts lie bleeding, waiting for the wind-
    loosed musk
Out of these tresses—the bright twist of black curls?

For what security have we here in this halting-place,
Where every moment the bell clangs "Strap up your packs"?

Stain your prayer-mat with wine if the Master tells you:
That seasoned voyager knows the ways of the road.

But traveling light, what can these land-lubbers know of it—
Black night, our fear of the waves, and the horrible whirlpool?

My self-willed love will sink my reputation:
The truth leaks out; they make a ballad of it at their meetings.

If you seek his presence, Hafiz, do not let him alone:
And when you meet his face, you can tell the world to go hang.

VII

(The return of Spring reawakens his passion. The orthodox may despise him, drunk with the wine of unreason. But such as he are the friends of God, and, like the Patriarchs, are under His protection.)

Again the garden has got the glitter of Spring:
The nightingale hears good news, for the rose is come.

Soft wind returning to the young plants of the meadow,
Greet for us the rose, the cypress and the sweet basil.

They are spread for the wedding-feast of the
    wine-seller's son,
And I'd sweep his floor with my eyelashes to win such grace.

For that amber-scented strand you draw across a
    moonlight brow
Has made a shuttlecock of my heart, and set it spinning.

I can't trust those who sneer at us drinking down to the lees:
That is the kind of thing which gets a bad name for religion.

Let them learn to be friends with God's true friends;
    remember that Noah in his ark,
A speck of dust himself, cared not a drop for the deluge.

Go out through the door of the house of Fate with its
    shifting spheres,
Nor drink of the sky's black bowl—it kills its guest at the last.

Tell those whose holding at length is no more than a
    fistful of dust:
"What need of these proud domes you rear to the sky?"

But as for you, you are Joseph, you are the Moon of Canaan:
The stewardship of Egypt is yours; so bid this prison
    good-bye.

Hafiz, drink wine, and be glad and reckless; but don't
    copy those
Who make reciting the Book a cover for lies.

VIII

(The beauty that he seeks seems ruthless and cruel, like the blond Turkish nomads. Utterly self-sufficient, it yet draws men to throw off all restraint, as did Potiphar's wife for the love of Joseph. But the mystery of the Universe cannot be solved with the intellect.)

If that Tartar, that fair-skinned Turk of Shiraz, gets hold
   of my heart
I'll give Bokhara and Samarkand for the Indian-black
   mole on his cheek.

Boy, hand me the wine that is left; for in Paradise
You won't find the waters of Ruknabad, or Musalla's
   rose-planted meadow.

Oh, but these handsome vagabonds, the town's marauders,
Snatch patience out of the heart as the Turks grab plunder
   on pay-day.

Such beauty has no need of our clumsy love:
No more than a lovely face needs pencil or makeup.

But let's talk of music and wine; leave probing the Universe:
That is a riddle which reason will never untie.

I know now how Joseph's beauty grew from day to day,
And her longing drove Zuleika into the open.

Though you give me harsh words, bad names, God's
    blessings upon you:
A bitter answer comes sweet on a sweet lip.

O my soul, receive this advice; to a lucky learner
More than his own soul is the Master's council.

You have made a poem, Hafiz, and threaded pearls; recite
    it deftly:
And on your verse Heaven scatter the knot of the Pleiades.

IX

(*Love's cruelty has driven him into the wilderness. Some show of gentleness might lure him back, but there is no trace of it in that face.*)

Soft wind, be kind, say to that slim gazelle:
"You have driven me out to the wastelands and the hills."

My compliments to that seller of all sweet things:
Does he not miss his parrot, his sugar-pecker?

Perhaps, O rose, your beauty makes you too proud
To be asking after the love-stricken nightingale?

Men of insight are taken captive by gentleness:
But you won't catch a clever bird with a trap or a wire.

A slender body, a dark eye, a countenance bright like the moon—
But why should these show no mark of kindness or friendship?

When you sit with the one you love and measure out the wine,
Remember the poor mad lovers who measure the winds.

Except for this one fault, I can find no flaw in your beauty—
But your face reveals no sign of truth or of love.

What wonder is there if catching the words of Hafiz
The song of the Morning Star sets the Messiah dancing!

XXIX

The post-boy wind that comes from the land of my Friend
Brings an amulet for the soul, the musk-scented screed of
    my Friend—

To show forth the splendor and the grace of my dear,
And tell of the majesty and magnificence of my Friend.

I gave him my heart to pay his pains for the message,
But I was ashamed to scatter such base coinage on behalf
    of my Friend.

Thank God, that with Fortune contriving all things for good,
His affairs are working together at the will of my Friend.

Here we are at his threshold, head bent in supplication:
Who might not thus sleep sound on the breast of his Friend?

What need for fear if slanderers draw breath against Hafiz?
Thank God, I'm not ashamed of my Friend!

XXXII

(*He will put no trust in this transitory world. The soul's true home is in the highest heaven—by the Sidra tree, where the Prophet had his revelation from the Angel Gabriel. But here below, there is no freedom but the knowledge of necessity.*)

Come, for our hopes are no more than a jerry-built house:
Bring wine, for life's foundations are rooted in wind.

But that man's zeal shall draw me, which under this blue ceiling
Burns bright for nothing that ties us down to the world.

How can I tell you what good news the angel of the Unseen
Brought me last night, flat-out on the wine-shop's floor?—

"O royal keen-eyed falcon, whose perch is on the Tree of Life,
Why is this corner of affliction's town your nest?

"They are whistling you home from the battlements of the Empyrean:
What could you be doing here in this place of snares?"

Take my advice, and follow out what I say—
This is a dictum the Master has handed down:

Don't let the world's ill harm you—(note this, a subtlety
From one who had traveled far upon love's way)—

But accept whatever is dealt you—unknit your brows:
We shall find no other way out; free choice is not ours.

Don't look to hold this tottering world to her bond:
She is the withered hag of a thousand bridegrooms.

There is no faith in the smile of the rose:
Lament, impassioned nightingale; there is room for complaint.

Why should poetasters be jealous of Hafiz?
To please by subtleties of speech is the gift of God.

XLIII

(He teaches the lover who complains of disdainful treatment how he must learn to suffer for love's sake. Beauty is transitory, and earthly glories pass like the legendary gardens of Iram and Jamshid's magic cup. Yet love remains—a reality that cannot be spoken, and a torment that it is impossible to conceal.)

At dawn's first breath the nightingale said to the opening rose:
"Less of the jilt, please; plenty like you have bloomed in this garden."

Laughing, the rose replied: "The truth won't vex me;
But no lover says harsh things to the one he loves.

"Tears, tears like pearls, must thread your eyelashes
Before you drink the wine from this jeweled cup;

"Nor love's perfume visit your longing sense
Till you've swept the tavern's threshold with your cheek."

Last night, when in the gardens of Iram
The gentle dawn-wind ruffled the hyacinth's tresses,

I said: "O throne of Jamshid, where now is his all-seeing cup?"
And came reply: "Alas, that vivid splendor sleeps."

The words of love fall short upon the tongue:
Boy, bring the wine; we'll speak of this no more.

Since Hafiz's tears swept prudence to the sea,
What shall he do? He cannot hide love's pain.

XLIV

With locks disheveled, flushed in a sweat of drunkenness,
His shirt torn open, a song on his lips and wine cup in hand—

With eyes looking for trouble, lips softly complaining—
So at midnight last night he came and sat at my pillow.

He bent his head down to my ear, and in a voice full of sadness
He said: "Oh my old lover, are you asleep?"

What lover, being given such wine at midnight,
Would prove love's heretic, not worshiping wine?

Don't scold us, you puritan, for drinking down to the dregs:
This fate was dealt us in God's Prime Covenant.

Whatever He poured into our tankard we'll swallow:
If it's liquor of Paradise, or the wine that poisons.

A laughing wine cup, a tangle of knotted hair—
And let good resolutions, like those of Hafiz, be shattered!

LXVII

(*He sets the beauty that he seeks against the world and its troubles. All the beauties of the world are but imperfect images of that. Taking the path of unreason, he has found his way to the fixed point that lies at the center of reality.*)

Your beauty, making common cause with virtue, has
 subdued the world:
Indeed, against such alliance, it could not stand.

When the candle was going to blab out the recluse's secret,
Thank God, its own dark heart put the check on its tongue.

The rose claimed the color and fragrance of the Friend,
And ardent, the morning breeze snatched its breath from
 his mouth.

The very sun is a spark that has flashed out into the sky—
Out from this hidden fire within my breast.

I stood on the edge of things, as on a circle inscribed,
But time's revolutions have borne me into the still center.

My life's harvest was burned when I fell in love with the
   wine bowl,
Catching the fire that gleamed from the image of the cup-
   bearer's cheek.

I gesture farewell; I go to the Magians' quarter,
Away from the troubles that catch at the skirts of the time.

Drink wine, for he who has seen how the world's business
   ends
Breaks through the turmoil unscathed, and lays hold on
   the cup for his prize.

In tulips' blood, on the rose's petal, they've written:
"The full-seasoned man takes wine, red like the
   judas-blossom."

Give wine in a golden cup; for our morning-draught, like
   a king
Has set the world to rout with a sword of gold.

Then seize your chance; since troubles have come on the
   world
Hafiz has taken to wine, and lets them go hang.

Since the waters of charity fall in drops from your song
How, Hafiz, can envious spirits carp at your words?

LXXIV

(Since reason is of no use to the lover, he must abandon himself to chance and to impulse. It lies in himself whether he shall prove to be of the chosen few who may achieve that perfect union which they seek.)

Knowing love's ocean is a shoreless sea,
What help is there?—abandon life, and founder.

Bring wine; don't scare us with Reason's prohibition:
That magistrate has no jurisdiction here.

When you give your heart to love, you make the moment lucky:
No need of auguries to perform good deeds.

Ask your own eye whose is the murderous glance;
O friend, this is not Fate's crime, nor the stars'.

Pure eyes discern him like the crescent moon;
But not all eyes have scope to see that splendor.

Seize the chance offered by the drunkard's road:
Like the clue on the treasure-track, not all can find it.

You are not moved, witnessing Hafiz's tears?
I cannot understand that heart, harder than stone.

LXXIX

No one has seen your face and there are a thousand
 watchers:
O rose, you are only a bud, and there are a hundred
 nightingales.

Small wonder if I, a stranger, have sought your company:
In this terrain there are legions of such as I.

Though I am far from you (and yet may no one be far!),
I live in the hope of an instant union with you.

Love knows no difference between monastery and
 drinking-booth,
For the light of the Friend's face irradiates all.

Where the business of the hermit's cell is transacted meetly,
Is the clapper of the Christians' sanctuary, and the name
 of the Cross.

Is there any lover whose state the Friend does not notice?
Sirs, there is no pain; if there was, we have a physician.

Not useless, after all, was this outcry of Hafiz,
But a most strange history, and a tale of marvels.

LXXX

In the snare of your locks the heart is its own tormentor:
Dispatch with a glance of your eye: this it has earned.

And if the soul's desire shall proceed from your hand,
Make speed in accomplishing that act of grace.

I swear by your own soul, sweet idol, like the midnight candle
My whole desire is to burn myself away.

When you purposed to love, I said, "O nightingale, desist:
For the rose that grows alone is for itself alone.

"The rose needs fetch no perfume from China or Turkestan,
For the belt of its own mantle encloses the bag of the musk."

Shun then the house of the niggardly lord of the time:
The treasure that brings you health rests in your own home.

Hafiz has burned away: he keeps to his own bond,
Where love makes the contract, and souls are put at hazard.

LXXXII

(*He sends the hoopoe (who was King Solomon's messenger to the Queen of Sheba) with greetings to his Friend, and receives in return an intimation that his homage is accepted. To find Truth, he has only to look into the mirror of his own heart.*)

O hoopoe flying on the dawn-wind, to Saba I am sending you:
Look, how far it is, from here to there, I'm sending you!

It's a pity—a bird like you in this dustbin of care:
To find the nest of fidelity I am sending you.

Say: *In love's road there is no far or near:*
I see you plain; my blessings I am sending you.

Morning and evening, cargoes of supplication
Upon the North and the East Wind I'm sending you.

Though you are hidden, my heart and you are friends:
Accept my compliments; praise I am sending you.

Lest grief's battalions should lay waste your heart
My own loved life for danegeld I am sending you.

To let musicians speak out my desire,
Poetry set in modes to the harmonica I am sending you.

Hand me the cup; good news speaks from the Unseen:
"Bear patiently the pain; here is a drug I am sending you.

"Enjoy God's craftsmanship in your own face
Revealed, as this reveals—the mirror I am sending you."

Hafiz, we sing your praise in our assemblies:
Hurry—a horse and a robe of honor I'm sending you.

XC

(*He complains of desertion for some more exalted lover.*)

O God-like beauty, who draws your veil aside?
O paradise-bird, who gives you water and seed?

Sleep's left my eyes, and the heart consumes away,
Wondering upon what breast your head is laid in sleep.

You suddenly left my breast, and my stricken heart:
Where have you found your home and your repose?

You have given no heed to all my bitter cries;
It is plain you have gone to some exalted place.

You make no inquiry after a wretch like me;
The needy finds nor pardon, nor recompense.

O palace that kindles the heart, O home of love,
God keep the calamity of days from ruining you!

In this wilderness the water hole is far:
Beware, lest the desert-phantom deceive with a mirage.

The arrow you shot from your glance went wide of the mark:
What fresh stratagem now will your malice conceive?

O heart, how will you find your way on the roads of old age?
In the days of your youth you went too much astray.

Your eye, the wine-seller, has found out the lover's heart:
It is plain enough that your liquor is strong poison.

Hafiz is not a runaway slave who deserts his master:
Come back, for your rebuke has broken me.

CXXI

(*In celebration of Spring, and of the poet's patron.*)

The rose has come into the garden, from Nothingness into Being,
And the violet bends down low at its feet in adoration.

Take your morning draft to the notes of the harp and the tambourine,
To the sound of the flute and the mandolin kissing the cup-bearer's throat.

Don't sit round the rose without wine, a beautiful youth and a harp,
For the days of our life are measured to a brief season.

Now the earth with its zodiac of herbs is as bright as the sky,
The star of good omens rising in favorable ascendant.

In the garden the tulip is kindled with Nimrod's furnace,
And we will renew that ancient cult of fire.

Take wine from the hand of the smooth-cheeked boy, miraculous-breathed as Jesus,
And retail me no more legends of the doom of infidel tribes.

The world grows like Paradise ever enduring, for the lily
    and rose come round:
But to what purpose do they?—nothing is permanent.

When the rose mounts up to the wind which Solomon rode,
There is a bird that rises with David's lament.

Call for a morning cup to the health of our modern Asaph—
King Solomon's minister, Imad ud-Din Mahmud—

So that Hafiz's companions may gain from his
    patronage—
And may he be prosperous in all that he undertakes!

CXXIII

(*He has been searching far and wide for the symbol of mystical truth. But (he is taught) it resides in the depths of his own heart. The Sufi martyr al-Hallaj was put to death because he proclaimed that he himself was the Truth; but his real offense was not blasphemy, but the indiscreet revealing of a profound mystery. The power of the Self works its false wonders, but for the truly enlightened man everything would be possible—even the miracles that Jesus did. But God veils Himself to restrain the ardor of His lovers.*)

For years my heart had been searching for Jamshid's
    magic cup,
Inquiring of strangers for its own perquisite;

Demanding from beachcombers on the ocean's fringe
A pearl which is outside the oyster of Space and Time.

Last night I took my perplexities to the old Magian,
Who had the insight to deal with mysteries.

I found him merry and laughing, a wine cup in his hand,
Enjoying the panorama reflected in its depths.

I said, "When did the Wise One give you this cosmic tankard?"
He answered, "When He enameled the vault of the sky.

"Poor sufferer—and God was with him all the time—
Who knew Him not, and deified remoteness.

"This juggling with the Selfhood—the Samaritan warlock
Faking the wonders of Moses' rod, and his white hand."

He said, "Our friend who ended on the gallows—
His only crime was this—blabbing of secrets.

"But if God's holy Angel would deign once more his grace,
Others might do the wonders Messiah worked."

I asked, "Why has my Love this strand of hair to bind me?"
"It is your lovesick heart, Hafiz, frets at that chain."

CLI

When the one I love takes a cup of wine in his hand
His beauty creates a slump in the market of idols.

Everyone who has seen the look in his eye is saying,
"Where's the police to put this drunkard in custody?"

I have tumbled like a fish into the ocean of love,
That he might come with a hook to haul me out.

I have fallen down at his feet in my deep affliction:
Will he be the one that will raise me up by the hand?

His heart is unburdened, who, like Hafiz, takes
A cup of wine as his covenanted destiny.

CXCIX

What good in being a solitary, secret drinker?
We're all drunkards together—let's leave it at that.

Unravel the heart's tangles, and leave the spheres alone:
You won't solve Fate's paradox by parallax.

Don't be surprised at Fortune's turns and twists:
That wheel has spun a thousand yarns before.

Respect the cup you hold—the clay it's made from
Was the skulls of buried kings—Bahman or Kobad.

For who can tell where Kai or Kaus are now,
Or Jamshid's throne, gone on a puff of wind?

Farhad dropped tears of blood for Shirin's lips,
And still I see the tulip blossoming there.

I think the tulip knows how Fortune cheats,
So clasps a petaled wine glass till it fades.

Come, let's get drunk, even if it is our ruin:
For sometimes under ruins one finds treasure.

The breeze of Musalla, the waters of Ruknabad,
They keep me still from wandering far from home.

Like Hafiz, drink your wine to the sound of harp-strings:
For the heart's joy is strung on a strand of silk.

CCXXII

(*The angels who created him from Adam's clay placed upon him the covenant of God's love. Therefore he remains steadfast, even though the final goal of love is annihilation.*)

Last night I saw that angels knocked upon the wine shop's door:
They took and tempered Adam's clay and formed a cup.

Those dwellers in the secret rooms of veiled chastity
Sprinkled the heady wine on me, lying there in the dust.

The sky could not sustain the burden of that trust:
They cast their lots, and pitched on me, whom love has crazed.

I thank God for the treaty between Him and me:
Dancing, celestial nymphs clinked glasses in gratitude.

How can we help but stray, with these hundred stooks of fantasy,
When wary Adam fell for one small grain?

Forgive the two-and-seventy sects their bickerings:
If they found truth, still could they follow vanity?

Love's fire's not that weak glimmer the candle laughs at,
But where the moth at last finds consummation.

The point of love murders the heart of him who sits retired,
Like the black mole that's stamped upon his darling's cheek.

None shall, as Hafiz does, withdraw Thought's veil,
Who has not combed out language, like a bride.

CCLXVIII

In the marketplace where they play tricks with the soul
They're crying something: "Listen, you dwellers in
    drunkard's alley, listen!

The daughter of the grape, absconded, missing, some days
    since!
Oyez, oyez, gather round, she's loose, look out!

"Dressed in a ruby frock, and wears a tiara of bubbles:
She's lifted reason and sense. Don't sleep, but be on your
    guard.

"Whoever brings back that bitter girl, I'll pay the price of
    her in sweets:
Go down and look for her in Hell, if she's hiding there!

"A fast one of the night, a thief, a rose-red bittersweet, a
    drunkard—
And if you find her, bring her to Hafiz's house."

CCCXLVIII

At dawn I came into the garden to catch a breath of the roses,
To cool my head for a little, like the nightingale sick with love.

I gazed upon the red rose in its glory,
Shining like a lamp that irradiates the darkness of night.

So proud it was of its beauty and its youth,
It could show all colors of disdain to the poor nightingale.

The narcissus lets fall a sorrowful tear from its eye:
Black-souled with grief, the heart of the tulip is marked
  with a thousand brands.

The iris shoots out its tongue, the sword of a rebel, against it:
The anemone gapes its mouth wide like a scandalmonger.

Here is a flower that lifts up a cup, like those whose
  worship is wine:
And one with a jug, like the youth who pours out for the
  drunkards.

Take your fill, like the rose, of revelry and all the lusts of
  youth:
Hafiz—the messenger needs only deliver his message.

CCCXXII

(*To praise the city of Shiraz, his birthplace, and of one who dwells there.*)

Oh my Shiraz, the nonpareil of towns—
The Lord look after it, and keep it from decay!

A thousand times God save the stream of Ruknabad
That makes us all immortal like the long-lived Khizr.

The North Wind's breath is rich with ambergris
That blows from Jafarabad to Mosalla.

Come to Shiraz, seek from her citizens
The grace of God's holy Angel: divine perfection girds them.

He'd waste his time bringing candy from Egypt
Here to this town, where everything is sweetness.

O West Wind blowing from one who is drunken and shiftless,
What news have you got for me?—how is he doing?

Even if he sheds my heart's blood—O my heart
Let it be lawful for him, as mother's milk to the child.

For the love of God, now I'm dreaming don't let me wake;
I'm happy enough with a fantasy of him.

Why, Hafiz, if you dread the parting of the ways,
Can't you be grateful for the times you had together?

CCCLV

Though a thousand enemies are making plans for my death,
So long as you are my friend I have no fear.

Hope of being one with you keeps me alive,
Or every moment apart would be filled with the fear of death.

Breath! breath! If I get no breath of him on the wind,
O time, O time! like the bursting rose I'll rip the collar
    from my throat.

Let my eyes never sleep till they gain the sight of you:
God's ban on the heart's patience while you are absent.

The wound that you give is better than another's salve:
If you give poison it is better than another's balm.

To die by the stroke of your blade is life eternal,
For my spirit is glad if it is your holocaust.

Don't swerve your horse aside; if you strike with your sword
I will give my head to dangle at your saddle-bow.

How can each eye behold you as you are?
Each comprehends according to his knowledge.

In the eyes of others Hafiz is the world's darling,
When his face is hidden in the dust before your dwelling.

CCCCXXXIX

(*This poem is inscribed on Hafiz's tomb at Shiraz.*)

Where is the news that makes me one with you—I would
 give up the ghost:
I am that paradisial bird whom the world's snares cannot
 hold.

By your love I swear it, if you give the summons to be
 your slave
I will soar beyond the dominions of Time and Space.

Send down, O my Lord, your rain from the guiding cloud,
Or I shift from the center of things like a speck of dust.

If you sit above my grave with music and wine
At the fragrance of you I shall rise from that narrow place
 and dance.

O exquisite image arise, show forth your form with its grace,
I will rise, and motion farewell to life and the world.

Though I am old, let me spend one night by your side,
And I shall arise at dawn with my youth renewed.

Give me one moment's relief at the hour of my death—
Like Hafiz, I shall escape from life and the world.

CCCCLVII

You monarch who keep your state with the box-tree's
    grace, king of sweet lips,
Your eyelashes break our spirits in the ranks whom love
    has routed.

He glanced, as the wine passed round, at me, a beggar,
And said, "You eye and luminary of eloquence,

"How long will your purse be empty of silver and gold?
Be my slave, and all silver bodies shall be for your pleasure.

"Are you less than a speck of dust? Rate yourself higher:
Be a lover, and make the riding sun your conquest.

"Nor lean on this paltry world: if you get a goblet of wine,
Take your fill of beautiful brows and delicate limbs."

My old wine-bibber—may his soul be happy—said:
"Keep out of the company of those who go back on their
    word.

"Catch the hem of your Friend's garment, break loose
    from the enemy:
Become God's man, have no truck with the legions of
    Ahriman."

I said to the morning breeze in the tulip-meadow:
"Who were the martyrs these bloody winding-sheets wrap?"

"Hafiz," it answered, "this is a mystery we are not
    permitted to know:
Let your talk be of wine like rubies and sweet lips."

CCCCLIX

The dawn is breaking, cup-bearer; fill up with wine:
The revolving heavens will not delay, so hurry!

Let us get drunk with a cup of the rose-red wine—
Before this transient world has itself passed out.

The sun of wine has risen upon the east of the bowl:
If pleasure is what you aim at, waste no time in sleep.

Since one day we'll be clay for Fate to make pitchers of,
Let my skull be a cup kept sweet, being filled with wine.

We are not bigots or puritans; we need no penance:
Preach to us only with a cup of the unmixed wine.

This worship of wine, Hafiz, is a virtuous business,
So be resolute in performance of righteous works.

CCCCLXXVII

(The sight of the sickle moon puts him in mind of the harvest of his own life. But if he can free himself from material ties, he need not despair. Earthly beauty is transitory, Fate carries all things away. But the smallest point of that true Beauty, which he seeks, can outweigh the lot. It is from this, not from the garb of conventional religion, that salvation is to be gained.)

I saw the green meadow of the sky and the sickle moon,
And remembered my own life's field and the time of harvest.

I said, "Oh my fate, while you slept, the sun has risen."
The answer came: "In spite of what's past, do not despair.

Go pure and naked like the Messiah to Heaven,
From your lamp a hundred beams shall reach the sun."

Don't trust your star, that sneak-thief of the night,
The trickster who stole the crown of Kaus, and the belt of Kaikhosrou.

Though gold and ruby bangles pierce your ears,
Attend the voice which tells how beauty fades.

Yet good luck to the mole which makes your face
   more lovely:
That little pawn can check the sun and moon.

And say to the sky, "Don't lay this trumpery out:
Love buys the moon for a barleycorn, and the
   clustered Pleiades for two."

The hypocrite's zeal makes religion a burnt harvest:
So burn your woolen cassock, Hafiz, and go!

CCCCLXXXIX

The lips of the one I love are my perpetual pleasure:
The Lord be praised, for my heart's desire is attained.

O Fate, cherish my darling close to your breast:
Present now the golden wine-cup, now the rubies of those
    lips.

They talk scandal about us, and say we are drunks—
The silly old men, the elders lost in their error.

But we have done penance on the pious man's behalf,
And ask God's pardon for what the religious do.

O my dear, how can I speak of being apart from you?
The eyes know a hundred tears, and the soul has a
    hundred sighs.

I'd not have even an infidel suffer the torment your beauty
    has caused
To the cypress which envies your body, and the moon
    that's outshone by your face.

Desire for your lips has stolen from Hafiz's mind
His evening lectionary, and reciting the Book at dawn.

DXVIII

Come, why should you be dealing harshly with me—
Something is due for our old companionship's sake.

Listen to a council which says, "The pearl of wisdom
Is better than any jewel you have in your safe."

But when will you reveal your face to the drunkard,
O you who hold the mirror of the sun and moon?

O reverend sir, don't call the wastrel wicked,
Or you fly in the face of God Who predestined him so.

Don't be afraid that my fiery sighs will scorch you—
You're safe enough, wrapped up in your holy cassock.

But help a poor soul made bankrupt by the morning after—
For God's love, if you've any of last night's wine still left!

Hafiz, I've not known verse that's so happy as yours—
As I swear by the Holy Book that you have in your heart.

DXXVIII

I went into the garden at dawn to gather roses,
When suddenly I heard the voice of the nightingale.

Poor thing, he was stricken in anguish for the love of the rose,
And sprinkled the meadows round with his sobs, as he looked for help.

Lost then in thought, slowly I paced in the garden,
Considering the affair of the rose and the nightingale.

The rose is become the image of Beauty, and the nightingale of Love:
The one will grant no favors, yet the other still remains constant.

When the voice of the nightingale prevailed upon my heart,
It seemed I had no power of endurance left.

For many roses have blossomed here in this garden,
But no one has plucked the rose without the stab of a thorn.

Hafiz, expect no relief from the turning heavens—
That wheel has a thousand flaws, and grants no favors.

Glossary of Names

Ahriman The principle of Evil in the Zoroastrian religion, opposed to Ormuzd (Ahura Mazda), the principle of Good.

Asaph According to the Moslem tradition, was vazir to King Solomon. He could understand the speech of birds.

Bahman An ancient legendary hero of Iran, identified with the Artaxerxes Longimanus of Greek and Roman writers, and also known in Persian as Ardishir Dirazdast. He has also been identified by some with the Ahasuerus of the Book of Esther.

Farhad The sculptor who became, according to the famous legend, enamored of Shirin, Khosrau Parviz's queen. He wandered disconsolately over the earth, carving her name, till the King came to an agreement with him that, if he cut a water channel through a mountain of rock, his suit would be considered. On hearing false news of Shirin's death, he committed suicide at the site of the digging.

Imad ud-Din Minister to Shah Abu Ishaq Inju, ruler of Shiraz (1341–1353). He is compared to Solomon's minister Asaf (the biblical Asaph).

Iram The garden planted by the legendary King Shadad, a descendant of Shem, in South Arabia. One commentator has it that Hafiz used a garden called Iram, belonging to his patron Shah Shuja. There is still a garden of this name in Shiraz.

Jafarabad A quarter to the east of Shiraz, now disappeared.

Jamshid An ancient king and culture-hero in Iranian legend (see Firdousi's *Shahnama*). He was believed to have possessed a magic cup, to which allusion is frequently made by Hafiz (see Introduction). This cup had the same property as the magic mirror of Alexander, as well as other mirrors in European medieval romances, of reflecting the whole world in its depths.

Jesus See Messiah.

Kai "Great King," probably refers to Kaikhosrou (*see* below).

Kaikhosrou The third Kayanian king.

Kaus, or Kaikaus The son of Kaikobad and the second king of the legendary Kayanian dynasty.

Khizr An important figure in Near Eastern folklore, the "Green Man" who had partaken of the water of the Fountain of Immortality. He has been variously identified with

Elijah, St. George, and Phineas, and is reputed to have been the Prophet's companion on the journey related in Koran, Surah VIII, verses 59–81. The Sufis believed in his immortal existence and periodic appearances at holy places. Green herbs were said to spring up where he had trodden.

Kobad The founder of the Kayanian dynasty of legend.

Messiah Jesus is regarded by Muslims as a man of infinite grace and the pattern of holiness. His miraculous powers are said to have resided in his breath.

Musalla A promenade near Shiraz, in which Hafiz found his last resting place.

Nimrod Abraham's persecutor and the reputed builder of the Tower of Babel. According to the Muslim Scripture (Koran, Surah XXI, verses 68, 69), Abraham was shot into a great fire by Nimrod's orders, and the fire miraculously turned into a field of flowers.

Ruknabad A canal at Shiraz, constructed by command of the Buyid prince Rukn ad-Dawla in A.D. 950, to irrigate the Shiraz plain.

Saba The name of the province referred to in the Koran, Surah XXVII, verse 21, containing the story of the hoopoe's message. It is the Sheba of the Bible.

Samaritan In the Koran, Surah XX, verse 87, the leading astray of the Jewish people during Moses' absence is attributed to one as-Samiri. This would appear to be an anachronism and it is suggested that Simon Magus, the man of Samaria, in Christian Scripture (Acts VIII, verses 9–24), might have been in the Prophet's mind; for this Simon, according to early Christian tradition, was the arch-heretic, who attempted to lead people astray from their religion and also practiced false magic.

Shirin The daughter, it is said, of the Byzantine Emperor Maurice and wife of Khosrau Parviz (A.D. 591). Farhad the Sculptor (q.v.) fell in love with her and on her account undertook to hew a way through a mountain of rock; but they were never united and their tale is one of tragedy.

Zuleika According to the Koran, the name of Potiphar's wife. The story of her love for Joseph forms a favorite subject for romance in the East, though no Arab woman is permitted to read the passage about Zuleika in the Koran.

Notes

VII, p. 27   "that amber-scented strand . . . has made a shuttlecock of my heart." The allusion in the original is to the game of polo.

VIII, p. 29   "the Turks grab plunder." A reference to the *Khan-i-yaghma*, "Feast of Spoil." It is said that on payday a feast was prepared for the Turkish soldiers, which they seized with mock-violence, perhaps to keep alive in their minds the source of their material benefits, i.e., the spoils of war.

Joseph is regarded as the type of masculine beauty throughout the Near East.

XXXII, p. 34   "the Tree of Life." Hafiz is referring to the *Sidra* or *Lote* tree, a sacred tree in the Muslim Paradise, beneath which Gabriel, the Angel of the Lord, was supposed to have communicated with the Prophet Mohammed.

"The Master." This, and similar phrases here and elsewhere, indicate the Magian Elder (*see* Introduction).

XLIV, p. 38 "Prime Covenant." The reference is to the contract between God and Man made when God created Man to bear the trust of Free Will, which the Angels, according to Muslim theology, had refused. God said to Man, "Am I not your Lord?" Man replied, "Yes," using the Arabic word *Bala*, which also means "calamity" in Persian. This covenant is referred to by Sufi poets as the covenant of *Alast*, from the first word of God's utterance, "*Alastu*," "Am I not?" The Koranic reference is Surah VII, verse 72. The Sufis took this primal covenant to be the origin of Man's desire to be reunited to God.

LXXXII, p. 46 According to the Koran, Surah XXVI, verse 21, the hoopoe was absent when Solomon looked for it, and came from a flight over Saba (Sheba) with news of the queen called Bilkis, with whom Solomon fell in love. "Danegeld." This word seemed to the translators to present the closest English analogy to the Persian word *nava*, taking that word in its rarer sense of "pledge," or "money sent to an invader to save a country from plunder."

CXXI, p. 50 "renew that ancient cult of fire." A daring reference, on the part of a Muslim poet, to Zoroastrianism.

"doom of infidel tribes." The original has a reference to the peoples of Ad and Thamud, legendary pre-Islamic tribes, destroyed by God on account of their wickedness.

CXXIII, p. 53 "our friend who ended on the gallows." The mystic Husain b. Mansur al Hallaj was put to death in A.D. 921 for blasphemy, having declared, "I am the Truth."

CXCIX, p. 55 "You won't solve Fate's paradox by parallax." Literally, "That is a puzzle that no mathematician can solve." Hafiz is evidently referring to the problems raised by the apparent discrepancies in the motions of the heavenly bodies in the Ptolemaic system.

CCXXII, p. 57 According to the Koran, the forbidden fruit for which Adam was cast out of Paradise was a grain of corn. For the two-and-seventy sects, see also FitzGerald's *Omar Khayyam*.

DXVIII, p. 73 "the Holy Book which you have in your heart." A reference to Hafiz's profession as a reciter of the Koran.